the
winter garden

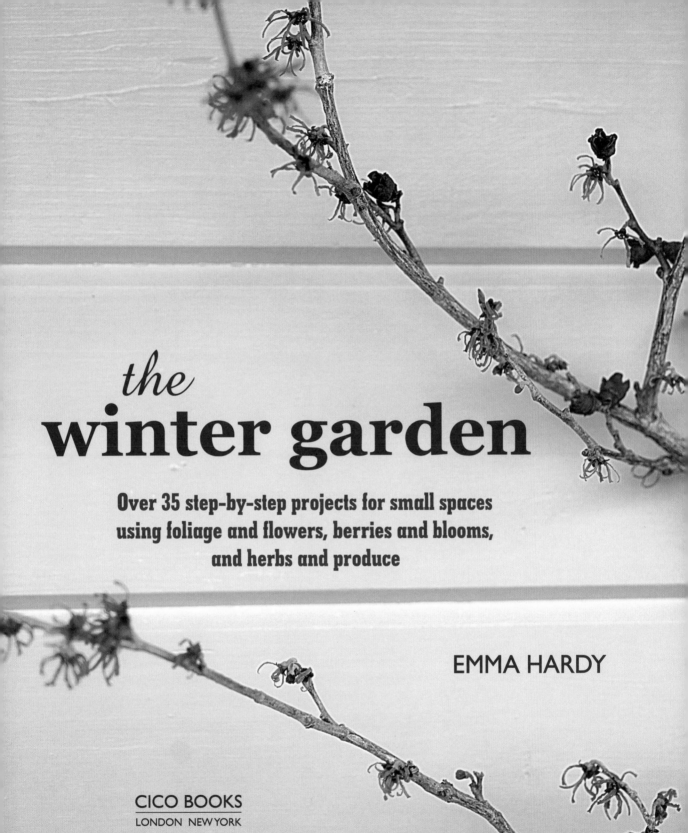

the
winter garden

Over 35 step-by-step projects for small spaces using foliage and flowers, berries and blooms, and herbs and produce

EMMA HARDY

CICO BOOKS
LONDON NEW YORK

Published in 2015 by CICO Books
An imprint of Ryland Peters & Small Ltd

20–21 Jockey's Fields   341 E 116th St
London WC1R 4BW   New York, NY 10029

www.rylandpeters.com

10 9 8 7 6 5 4 3 2 1

Text © Emma Hardy 2015
Design and photography © CICO Books 2015

A CIP catalog record for this book is available from the Library
of Congress and the British Library.

ISBN: 978 1 78249 238 2

Printed in China

Editor: Gillian Haslam
Designer: Luana Gobbo
Photographer: Debbie Patterson
Stylist: Emma Hardy

In-house designer: Fahema Khanam
Art director: Sally Powell
Production controller: David Hearn
Publishing manager: Penny Craig
Publisher: Cindy Richards

contents

introduction

The garden can feel like a neglected space in winter, but there are so many plants that look wonderful throughout this season that it is a shame not to include some of them in your garden, especially to make the best of pots and containers. Shape, texture, and foliage are important elements in the winter garden when flowers can be few and far between and, as much as I love spring and summer flowers for their colors and scents, winter plants have their own special appeal.

So here are lots of ideas for containers to brighten up your outside space, from colored berries in an old galvanized bin to elegant grasses in a metal trunk and pretty pansies, daffodils, and ivy in tiered enamel tubs. Indoor containers are a must over winter, too, and poinsettias displayed in a group, amaryllis with moss and ivy, and forced bulbs in metal dishes will all be welcome in your home. Edible winter

harvests, such as a windowbox planted with evergreen herbs or beautiful cabbages grown with thyme and sage, are also well worth considering and can make attractive displays as well as providing food. Each project gives you a plant list and step-by-step instructions, which can also be used to inspire you to create your own planting ideas.

Winter gardening has an added advantage that generally plants require little attention over the cold months—apart from deadheading pansies and cyclamen, your planted containers will look after themselves very well. Winter planting also means that you can cram lots of plants into pots to create abundant displays, as they will not need as much room to grow as during spring and summer months.

All the projects can be created with just a few basic gardening tools and very little experience. I hope that most of the plants I have used will be available from your local garden centers and nurseries, although the many online nurseries available to us now mean that sourcing plants should not be a problem. Look out for unusual containers and pots, too—anything from old buckets and tubs to metal trunks and vintage wooden crates—in markets and car boot sales.

Winters vary greatly from region to region, from mild, damp weather to freezing, snowy conditions, so bear this in mind when planning your garden planting. Get advice from local growers to find out what will grow and thrive in your area or zone.

When you have planted your winter containers, make sure that you take time to enjoy them. I am always surprised to spot the first hellebore flowers appearing in my garden and delighted to find snowdrop and iris leaves emerging through bare soil. I hope this book will inspire you to create beautiful pots and containers to brighten up your garden over winter and beyond, and to consider gardening in winter as a worthwhile and enjoyable activity that doesn't need to take a back seat.

basic *techniques*

When planting up containers for winter, it is important to consider and prepare well so that your winter displays will look good for as long as possible. Here are a few tips and techniques to help you get the best out of your pots and plants.

Choosing a container

There is a huge selection of pots and containers available from garden centers, plant nurseries, and DIY stores, from classic terra cotta and colorful ceramic pots to wooden boxes and plastic troughs and tubs. Choosing containers is really a matter of taste, so looking for colors, shapes, and textures that you really love will help you create beautiful planting displays.

Terra cotta looks great and gets better with age, although it can be prone to frost damage, which can cause pots to crack or chip. If you get particularly cold winters, it may be best to reserve your terra cotta pots for summer planting and simply store them indoors during winter months. If buying new terra cotta pots, check that they are frost-proof so that they will not crack in very cold weather.

Glazed pots can add a splash of color to the winter garden, but, as with terra cotta, check that they are fully hardy and will not suffer in cold weather. Plastic pots are a very practical choice and have the added benefit that they can often be bought cheaply, but personally, I think they lack charm and I prefer to scour flea markets for unusual and usually very cheap alternatives. Look around for old buckets, enamel pots, and metal trunks (metal being particularly hardy in cold weather). Stone containers are also very sturdy, making them great winter containers.

If it is possible to make drainage holes in a container (see right) and if it is weatherproof, it will be possible to use it as a garden planter, so consider all sorts of containers and boxes and think about how you could plant them up. The projects that follow will give you inspiration.

It is important to use clean containers for planting to help reduce pests and diseases. Wash or scrub the containers with warm soapy water, rinse them well, and dry thoroughly before planting them up.

above left: A collection of pretty enamel tubs.

above right: Ceramic pots work well for winter planting.

Drainage holes

It is important to make sure that containers have adequate drainage. Store-bought planters and pots usually have at least one hole in the bottom, but if using old buckets and tubs you may need to make holes yourself. Use a hammer and nail (or drill with a suitable bit if something more heavy-duty is needed) and make a few holes across the base of the container so that excess water will drain away.

Adding crocks

Pieces of terra cotta pots, tiles, and broken china can be used as drainage crocks. Place them over drainage holes in the base of your containers to prevent the holes becoming blocked with potting compost. Break up the pots, tiles, or china carefully with a hammer and keep any excess bits to use in future planting. If any of your terra cotta pots have cracked during a previous winter, save the pieces.

Insulating pots

Most of the plants used in this book will withstand low temperatures, but it can be useful to insulate pots if the plants are more susceptible to frost damage (your local garden center will be able to advise on this). Lining the inside of a pot with bubble wrap or adding broken pieces of polystyrene before planting can help to insulate the container.

If leaving terra cotta pots outside over winter, covering the outside of the pot with bubble wrap will provide some protection from frosts. As bubble wrap is not particularly pretty, wrap the pot in a piece of burlap or hessian, tied with a length of twine or raffia.

Siting your containers

Some plants, although suitable for winter containers, may prefer a sheltered spot, and

above: Make sure pots have adequate drainage.

right: Old metal food molds make great indoor planters.

generally, containers positioned near the house will benefit from the warmer, less windswept location. Think about a suitable position for your containers, making sure that you will be able to see and enjoy them throughout winter. Placing them near your front door or in view of the kitchen window is always a good option.

If your containers are sited in a spot prone to flooding or puddles, you could raise the pots off the ground by sitting them on "feet."

Choosing plants

When making up winter planters, carefully consider which plants to use so that they have the best possible chance to thrive. Think about the size and scale of each plant, and consider how severe the winters usually are in your region or gardening zone. Your local garden center or nursery will be able to advise you which plants are best suited to your winter weather conditions and temperatures.

Take plants out of their pots to check their roots before buying, to make sure they are not pot bound and are free from pests and diseases.

below left: Loosen roots gently before planting.
below center: Adding grit or sand will improve drainage.
right: Check containers regularly and water as necessary.

below left: Loosen roots gently before planting.
below center: Adding grit or sand will improve drainage.
right: Check containers regularly and water as necessary.

Always soak plants before planting them in their new containers. Immerse the root ball in a bowl or bucket of water for at least 20 minutes or until the potting compost and root ball are completely wet.

Loosening the roots

Sometimes plants that have been in their pots for a long time can become root bound. Before replanting them, take them out of their pots and carefully pull and tease the roots a little with your fingertips. This will encourage them to grow and spread out in their new containers. Take care not to damage the roots while teasing them.

Choosing potting compost

Your local garden center or nursery probably stocks a range of different potting composts and potting mixes. Winter containers have relatively simple requirements when it comes to their growing medium. Most of the plants used in this book will be happy in good-quality multi-purpose potting compost as over-wintered plants do not need high levels of nutrients (unlike spring and

summer plants that will grow substantially). If planting shrubs and small trees for a long-term container, select a soil-based potting compost to encourage root growth and give your plants a good start. If possible, choose peat-free potting compost as this is more environmentally friendly.

Ericaceous potting compost can be used for lime-hating plants, such as heathers or witch hazels, which prefer a pH level of less than 7. However, I usually find that even lime-hating plants are fine over winter in a good-quality multi-purpose potting compost, so unless you are creating long-term planting, ericaceous potting compost probably will not be necessary.

When planting bulbs for indoors, bulb fiber can be used. This is light and has good drainage, which reduces the risk of bulbs sitting in very wet potting compost, which would cause them to rot.

Adding grit or sand

Most plants will not like sitting in very wet compost or soil, which can be a problem over winter. Adding a few handfuls of horticultural grit or sand to the potting compost and putting a layer of gravel in the bottom of a pot can both help to improve drainage and prevent the roots rotting. Vermiculite and perlite, which should both be available from your local garden center, can be added and will also help to improve drainage, but can be slightly more expensive.

Watering and feeding

In winter, watering of planted containers needs to be reduced as potting compost can easily become too wet. For the most part, plants do not like to sit in compost that is waterlogged as it may cause the roots to rot and can increase the risk of the potting compost and roots freezing in very cold weather.

Containers that are sited in open areas and will catch rainfall are unlikely to need any additional watering, although it is a good idea to check the potting compost in pots every now and then, especially if your winters are dry. If leaves and petals look very droopy, dry, or discoloured, the container may well need watering. However, evergreens can be hard to gauge as the foliage can look fine but the roots can be suffering damage, so sticking your fingers into the potting compost to check the moisture level is a good idea.

Potting compost in pots and containers should be kept moist but not too wet, and you should avoid letting the compost dry out regularly and then flooding it with water. Aim for a fairly steady level of moisture and your plants will look their best and live happily in their pots.

Feeding plants with fertilizer is not necessary during winter as they will survive quite happily through their dormant season on the nutrients in the potting compost. Using a liquid fertilizer or adding controlled-release fertilizer pellets is recommended from spring through summer as the plants in containers will require additional nutrients to help them grow and thrive.

Maintenance

Winter containers are much more low maintenance than their summer counterparts and will usually look after themselves. Apart from checking the moisture of the potting compost, very little will be required of you— although a quick check every few weeks will make sure that you spot any problems early.

Deadheading, which means picking off the dead flower heads to encourage more blooms, is a good idea for winter bedding plants such as pansies, violas, and cyclamen. Checking at least weekly will help the plants to keep flowering so that your containers look good for longer.

After winter

If plants are staying in their containers once winter is over, it is good to refresh the potting compost (remove the top layer of old compost and adding new compost), incorporating fertilizer pellets to encourage new growth.

Remove winter bedding plants when they are past their best, replacing them with spring and summer flowers to keep the display going. In containers where the plants are packed in (as most of mine are!), it may be a good idea to remove one or two of them and replant in new containers so that each plant has more growing room.

When bulbs have finished flowering, leave the flower heads in place for about five weeks, then cut them off. Either replant the bulbs out in your garden or take the bulbs out of their potting compost and let them dry out, ready to replant the following fall.

right: Deadhead pansies to keep them flowering.

plants for *winter*

The following lists of plants will all add something to your winter garden, providing color and form, fragrance, flowers, and even food. Use the lists as a guide to help you choose plants for your containers or garden. Before buying any plants, it is a good idea to talk to staff at your local garden center or plant nursery, who should be able to advise you about what will grow well in your area and provide you with information about how hardy plants will be in your part of the country or gardening zone. Check also that plants will suit the size of your containers or gardens, as some plants listed here will be better suited to larger gardens.

below: Succulents can look good throughout the winter season.
below right: Clematis flowers are a welcome addition to the winter garden.

FOLIAGE AND COLOR

Aucuba japonica (spotted laurel)

Brassica oleracea (ornamental cabbage)

Chamaecyparis lawsoniana (Lawson's cypress)

Choisya ternata (Mexican orange blossom)

Cornus (dogwood)

Cryptomeria japonica (Japanese cedar)

Cupressus macrocarpa (Monterey cypress)

Eucalyptus gunii (cider gum tree)

Euonymus fortunei (spindle)

Euphorbia (spurge)

Fatsia japonica (castor oil plant)

Hamamelis x intermedia (witch hazel)

Hebe (veronica)

Hedera helix (ivy)

Heuchera (coral flower)

Heucherella

Juniperus (juniper)

Leucothoe scarletta (dog hobble)

Pittosporum tenuifolium (New Zealand pittosporum)

Salix alba (golden willow)

Senecio cineraria (silver ragwort)

WINTER SCENT

Chimonanthus praecox (wintersweet)

Clematis cirrhosa var. *balearica* (fern-leaved clematis)

Coronilla valentina subsp. *glauca* 'Citrina'

Daphne bholua (Nepalese paper plant)

Hamamelis x intermedia (witch hazel)

Hyacinthus orientalis (hyacinth)

Iris unguicularis (Algerian iris)

Jasminum nudiflorum (winter jasmine)

Narcissus (daffodil, particularly 'Paper White')

Sarcococca confusa (sweet box)

Viburnum x bodnantense (arrowwood)

WINTER BERRIES

Callicarpa bodinieri (beauty berry)

Cotoneaster

Ilex (holly)

Pernettya mucronata
(prickly heath)

Pyracantha (firethorn)

Solanum pseudocapsicum
(winter cherry)

WINTER FLOWERS

Amaryllis

Bellis perennis (daisy)

Calluna vulgaris (heather)

Clematis cirrhosa 'Jingle Bells'

Clematis urophylla 'Winter Beauty'

Crocus

Cyclamen hederifolium (cyclamen)

Daphne mezereum
(white mezereon)

Epimedium (barrenwort)

Eranthis hyemalis (winter aconite)

Erica carnea (heather)

Euphorbia pulcherrima
(poinsettia)

Galanthus (snowdrop)

Helleborus niger (Christmas rose)

Hyacinthus orientalis (hyacinth)

Iris reticulata

Jasminum nudiflorum (jasmine)

Lonicera x *purpusii*
'Winter Beauty' (honeysuckle)

Mahonia x *media*
(lily-of-the-valley bush)

Muscari armeniacum
(grape hyacinth)

Narcissus (daffodil)

Polyanthus (primula)

Sarcococca confusa (sweet box)

Skimmia japonica

Viburnum tinus (laurustinus)

Viola x *wittrockiana* (pansy)

WINTER BULBS

Amaryllis

Crocus

Cyclamen hederifolium
(cyclamen)

Eranthis hyemalis (winter aconite)

Galanthus (snowdrop)

Hyacinthus orientalis (hyacinth)

Iris reticulata

Iris unguicularis (Algerian iris)

Muscari armeniacum
(grape hyacinth)

Narcissus (daffodil)

WINTER FERNS

Asplenium scolopendrium
'Angustifolia' (hart's tongue fern)

Asplenium trichomanes
(maidenhair fern)

Dryopteris filix-mas
(male fern)

Pteris cretica 'Rowerii'
(ribbon fern)

Selaginella kraussiana 'Gold Tips'
(Krauss' gold tips)

Woodwardia unigemmata
(walking fern)

WINTER GRASSES

Acorus gramineus
(slender sweet flag)

Carex comans 'Bronze'
(New Zealand hair grass)

Festuca glauca (blue fescue)

Miscanthus sinensis (eulalia)

Ophiopogon planiscapus
'Nigrescens' (black mondo)

Stipa tenuissima
(Mexican feather grass)

Uncinia rubra (red hook sedge)

WINTER HERBS

Laurus nobilis (bay tree)

Origanum vulgare (oregano)

Petroselinum crispum (parsley)

Rosmarinus officinalis (rosemary)

Salvia officinalis (sage)

Thymus vulgaris (thyme)

WINTER VEGETABLES

Brussels sprouts

Cabbages

Cavolo nero

Fava/broad beans

Garlic

Leeks

Onions

Purple sprouting broccoli

Sorrel

Spinach

Swiss chard

Winter lettuce (such as rouge
d'hiver, lamb's lettuce, winter
purslane, land cress)

right: Ivy works well in winter
planters and can withstand very
low temperatures.

chapter 1
stems & leaves

splendid *succulents*

These low-lying succulents in a variety of colors in a shallow concrete planter make a wonderful miniature winter garden. All the plants, apart from *Echeveria* 'Magic Red,' can withstand low temperatures, so if your container will be sited in an unsheltered spot, it may be worth substituting it for a more hardy variety.

YOU WILL NEED

Shallow dish with a drainage hole

Crocks

Gravel

Potting compost, with a few handfuls of sand added for drainage

Selection of succulents—I used *Sedum oregonense* (cream stonecrop), *Sedum acre* 'Minus' (biting stonecrop), *Sedum spathulifolium* 'Purpureum'

(purple stonecrop), *Sedum rubrotinctum* (banana cactus), *Euphorbia myrsinites* (broad-leaved glaucous spurge), *Echeveria runyonii* 'Topsy turvy,' and *Echeveria* 'Magic Red'

Paintbrush

Decorative gravel

1 Cover the drainage hole in the dish with a couple of crocks so that it will not become clogged with potting compost.

2 Add a thick layer of gravel—¾ in (2cm) deep should be adequate—spreading it out evenly over the bottom of the dish.

3 Put the potting compost and sand mixture into the dish, half filling it. Press down lightly to make sure that there are no air pockets.

4 Soak the plants in water for about 10 minutes and remove from their pots. Start to position the plants in the dish, removing a little of the potting compost if the root balls are very large.

5 Continue moving the plants around until you are happy with the arrangement. Use trailing plants near the edge so that they will spill out of the container.

6 Add handfuls of the potting compost mixture around the plants to fill in any gaps, trying to avoid compost falling on to the plants. When all the gaps are filled, press the surface of the compost slightly and flatten it.

7 Using a paintbrush, carefully brush off any loose potting compost from the plants, as it can often fall into the crevices.

8 Spread decorative gravel over the surface of the compost, again trying to avoid it falling on the plants (the gravel helps to protect the plants during very cold weather). Water the container and leave to drain.

AFTERCARE

The plants used here will look good throughout the year, but some are frost tender. If your winters are frosty, keep the dish in a sheltered spot, bringing it indoors if the weather is very cold. Keep the potting compost slightly damp, but do not overwater.

metal hanging *planter*

This unusual metal planter with pockets is perfect for small plants, creating an eye-catching display. Vertical fabric hangers are also readily available from garden centers, or try hanging small pots on nails, positioning them in columns for a similar look.

1 This hanger has a drainage hole at the bottom of each pocket, but if your container does not, add a few using a nail and hammer. Put a few scoops of potting compost into a pocket of the hanger, pressing it down a little to remove air pockets. As the planting pockets are small, adding a little grit to the compost before planting should create enough drainage for the plants.

2 Soak the plants in water for at least 20 minutes to ensure the roots are wet. Take a plant from its pot, loosen the roots a little, and place in the pocket, adding more potting compost around it if necessary. If the root ball is too large to fit in a pocket, scrape some of the compost from the root ball, making sure not to damage the roots. Fill the other pockets with plants in the same way, arranging them so they splay outward and downward. Water each pocket of the hanger, ensuring that the potting compost is damp rather than wet.

YOU WILL NEED

Metal hanging planter

Potting compost

Horticultural grit

Dryopteris erythrosora 'Prolifica' (lacy autumn fern)

Hedera helix (ivy)

Leptinella squalida 'Platt's Black' (black brass buttons)

Artemisia vulgaris 'Oriental Limelight' (variegated wormwood)

Lonicera nitida 'Baggesen's Gold' (poor man's box)

AFTERCARE

Keep an eye on the hanger, watering every couple of weeks or whenever necessary, especially if the hanger is under cover or in sun.

family of *ferns*

Many ferns look beautiful all year round and so are perfect for winter. Choose plants that are evergreen, varying the colors and textures for an interesting display. An old sink has been used to create this little fern garden, which highlights the plants well and provides enough room for the ferns to thrive.

YOU WILL NEED

Old belfast sink

Crocks

Pieces of polystyrene (the containers plants come in are ideal)

Potting compost

Selection of ferns—I used *Woodwardia unigemmata* (walking fern), *Asplenium trichomanes* (maidenhair fern),

Asplenium scolopendrium 'Angustifolia' (hart's tongue fern), *Pteris cretica* 'Rowerii' (ribbon fern), *Selaginella kraussiana* 'Gold Tips' (Krauss' gold tip spikemoss), and *Dryopteris filix-mas* (male fern)

Pieces of decorative bark

1 Make sure that the sink's plug hole is not blocked, as ferns do not like to sit in very wet soil. Cover the hole with crocks, adding more to cover the base of the sink. This will help with drainage.

2 Break up the polystyrene and place in the sink. This is a cheap and effective way of filling a large container and will reduce the amount of potting compost needed. It will also help to insulate the container.

3

4

5

3 Half-fill the container with potting compost, leveling it out and making sure that there are no air pockets around the pieces of polystyrene.

4 Soak the root balls of the plants in water for about 20 minutes to make sure that they are moist. Take a fern from its pot and place it in the sink.

5 Continue to plant the other ferns, moving them around if necessary to form a pleasing arrangement. Use the taller plants at the back with the smaller, denser ones toward the front.

6 Add a few pieces of decorative bark to the sink, covering any areas of potting compost—this will give an attractive woodland look to the container.

6

AFTERCARE

Ferns are fairly hardy, but they prefer a slightly sheltered spot out of the wind. They will thrive in damp but not wet soil, so providing good drainage is important. Additional watering should not be necessary unless the container is under cover.

a trunk of *grasses*

The inspiration for this project came from the lovely color of the rusty old trunk I bought from a yard sale. Grasses in shades of brown and gold complement the deep orangey color of the metal, introducing an unusual color scheme to the winter garden. Grasses feature highly in winter gardens because, although they lose some of their color, they keep their shape throughout the season, adding interesting form to containers and border planting. The heuchera was added as its color was so beautiful, but it could easily be omitted if you would prefer to plant only grasses.

YOU WILL NEED

Old metal trunk

Large nail

Hammer

Crocks

Potting compost

Coarse gravel

Pennisetum x *advena* 'Rubrum' (red fountain grass)

Pennisetum setaceum 'Rubrum' (purple fountain grass)

Stipa arundinacea (pheasant's tail grass)

Carex comans (bronze New Zealand hair grass)

Heuchera 'Marmalade' (coral bells)

1 Make holes in the bottom of the trunk if it does not have any, using a large nail and hammer. Jiggle the nail in the holes a little to make them as big as possible.

2 Cover the bottom of the trunk with the crocks to help with drainage and to prevent the holes becoming blocked with potting compost.

3 Half-fill the trunk with potting compost, adding a few handfuls of gravel as you go to help drainage.

4 Soak all the plants in water for at least 20 minutes so that the root balls are completely wet. Take the red fountain grass from its pot and place at the back of the trunk, loosening the roots slightly with your fingers to encourage them to spread.

5 Plant the red fountain grass next to it in the same way. Then plant the pheasant's tail grass in the front of the trunk, and squeeze the bronze New Zealand hair grass next to it, leaving some space on the left-hand side.

6 Take the heuchera from its pot and plant in the remaining gap, adding more potting compost around all the plants to fill in any gaps and hold them all in place.

AFTERCARE

These grasses prefer a frost-free spot, so position the trunk near the house
or in a sheltered area. Do not overwater as the pennisetum in particular may
rot if sitting in very wet soil. Cut the grasses back in early spring for a fresh
display throughout the year.

tabletop *trough*

Miniature spruce trees form the centerpieces for these sweet table decorations. Rusty metal boxes have each been planted up with a tiny tree, mind-your-own-business, and bead plants, with bun moss added to create little gardens. Adding a star decoration gives a Christmassy touch (it's easy to make one from craft foil).

YOU WILL NEED

Old metal box

Gravel

Potting compost

Miniature *Picea glauca* conica (white spruce)

3 x small *Soleirolia soleirolii* (mind-your-own-business)

3 x small *Nertera granadensis* (bead plant)

Bun moss (available from floristry suppliers)

Silver star (optional)

1 Making holes in the bottom of the box will help with drainage (see page 26). However, if your box is for a dining table, remember to use a tray underneath it to prevent damage to the surface of the table. Alternatively, leave the box without holes and water sparingly, taking care not to overwater. Add a thick layer of gravel along the bottom of the box. Level the surface of the gravel.

2 Half-fill the box with potting compost and level the surface.

3 Soak the root balls of the plants in water for about 10 minutes until they are completely wet. Take the spruce from its pot, loosening the roots a little if necessary, and plant in the middle of the box, pushing it down into the potting compost so that the surface of the root ball sits below the rim of the box.

4 Take a mind-your-own-business plant from its pot and scrape away some of the soil from the roots so that it will sit flat in the box. Plant in one corner of the box so that the foliage sits just above the rim of the box.

5 Remove a bead plant from its pot and carefully remove some of the soil from the roots. Plant along the other side of the box, leaving a gap next to the mind-your-own-business.

6 Continue to plant the remaining plants along the box randomly, leaving a few gaps for the bun moss.

7 Fill in around the plants with potting compost so they are tightly held in place. Add a piece of bun moss next to the mind-your-own-business and bead plants. Using a little potting compost underneath the bun moss will enable it to sit at the same level as the plants.

AFTERCARE

Water the box once planted. Make sure you check the potting compost regularly and water if it feels dry. Keep the bun moss damp to prevent it losing its bright green color. The spruce will need regular watering as it will not like drying out.

8 Fill in any remaining gaps with a little potting compost and smaller pieces of bun moss so there are no gaps and none of the compost can be seen.

skimmia and *stone*

Classic stone urns work well in any garden and they can withstand the harshest of winters without damage. This planting uses bold plants in contrasting colors, with the skimmia adding a lovely pink and the fern softening the overall look. This is an ideal maintenance-free container as, apart from checking the moisture of the potting compost, it can be left to its own devices.

YOU WILL NEED

Large stone urn

Crocks

Potting compost

Skimmia japonica 'Rubella'

Heuchera obsidian (coral bells)

Euphorbia amygdaloides 'Ruby Glow' (wood spurge)

Lonicera nitida 'bagensen's Gold' (poor man's box)

Dryopteris filix-mas (male fern)

1 Cover the drainage hole in the bottom of the urn with a couple of crocks to prevent the hole becoming blocked with potting compost.

2 Half-fill the urn with potting compost, spreading it out evenly.

3 Soak the root balls of all the plants in water for about 20 minutes until they are completely wet. Remove the skimmia from its pot and gently pull the roots to loosen them slightly. Plant it in the urn, positioning it to one side.

4 Take the heuchera from its pot and plant next to the skimmia, again loosening the roots if they are pot bound.

5 Remove the euphorbia from its pot and plant in the sink, pushing it into the urn so that the root balls of all three plants are level and do not sit higher than the rim of the urn.

6 Plant the lonicera by removing it from its pot and tucking it into the urn in front of the skimmia. Again, make sure that the surface of the soil is level. Add a few handfuls of potting compost around the plant, leaving enough room for the last plant.

7 Plant the fern in the same way, and fill around the plants with additional potting compost if necessary so there are no holes.

AFTERCARE

This is a very hardy container that will require little maintenance. The plants will more or less look after themselves, although it is a good idea to check the potting compost during dry spells and water it if necessary.

wreath of *succulents*

This beautiful living wreath is very simple to make and will look good all year round. Succulents are tough plants and cope well when divided, rooting well when replanted. I've used a large selection of plants, but if they are not available at your garden center or you wish to keep the cost down, simply break off sections from succulents you already have. Try to vary the colors from greens and whites to reds and mauves.

YOU WILL NEED

Moss (available from florists)

Wire wreath base, 14 in (35cm) in diameter

Potting compost

Copper wire

Selection of succulents—I used *Jovibarba hirta neilreichii*, *Jovibarba heuffelii*, *Sedum acre* 'Golden Queen,' *Sedum* 'Alba,' *Sedum* 'Sakhalin,' *Saxifraga* 'Southside

Seedling,' *Delosperma congestum* 'Golden Nugget,' *Lewisia tweedyi*, *Sempervivum* 'Fuego,' *Rhodiola pachyclados*, *Chiastophyllum oppositifolium*, and *Androsace sempervivoides*

Stiff floristry wire

Wire cutters

1 Tear the moss into pieces and lay them in a ring shape slightly larger than the wire wreath base, root side up, on the table. Lay the wire wreath base on top of the moss.

2 Place handfuls of potting compost on the wire wreath base. Gather up the moss to cover the base and potting compost completely, wrapping copper wire around it to hold it in place.

3

4

5

3 Cut a length of copper wire about 20 in (50cm) long and fold it in half. Wrap it around what will be the top of the wreath, twisting it around itself to form a loop to act as a hanger.

4 Gently pull florets and sections of the succulents from their main plants, keeping the roots intact. Cut the floristry wire into lengths of about 4 in (10cm) and bend them in half to form a "U" shape. Dig a small hole in the moss with your finger and lay the plant in it, securing it in place by pushing a bent wire around the base of it. This will be easier with some succulents than others, but judge each one individually, adding an additional wire if you need to.

5 Work around the wreath, adding more plants and varying the shapes and colors to form an attractive arrangement. Leave little gaps between plants so they will have room to grow and fill the space. Check that all the plants, the potting compost, and the moss are securely held in place by the wire. Wind the wire around itself a few times to fasten it and cut with wire cutters.

AFTERCARE

Ideally, the wreath should be left lying horizontal for at least a couple of weeks to give the plants a chance to root themselves, but if you are making it at the last minute to decorate a party, ensuring that the plants are tightly held in place should be enough to keep it looking good when it is hanging. Succulents can survive quite dry conditions, so make sure that the wreath does not become waterlogged. In very dry weather, just moisten the moss and potting compost a little.

hanging basket of *heucherellas*

Hanging baskets usually make me think of summer when they are planted up with floral bedding plants, but this striking basket with heucherellas and heuchera in subtle colors will survive freezing temperatures and look good all year round. The heucherellas will tumble beautifully out of the basket as the plants grow.

YOU WILL NEED

Hanging basket with liner

Potting compost (add water-retaining granules if the basket will be hung in a sunny spot, to help prevent it drying out)

Sharp craft or DIY knife

Old newspaper

Heucherella 'Gold Cascade,' 'Copper Cascade,' 'Sweet Tea,' and 'Burnished Bronze'

Heuchera 'Marmalade' (coral bells)

3 x *Muehlenbeckia axillaris* (creeping wire vine)

2 x *Hedera helix* (ivy)

1 Place the liner inside the hanging basket and stand the basket on top of a plant pot or bucket to keep it stable. Half-fill the basket with potting compost, spreading it out evenly.

2 Using the knife, cut a slit in the liner about 4 in (10cm) long, making sure that you keep the rim of the liner intact.

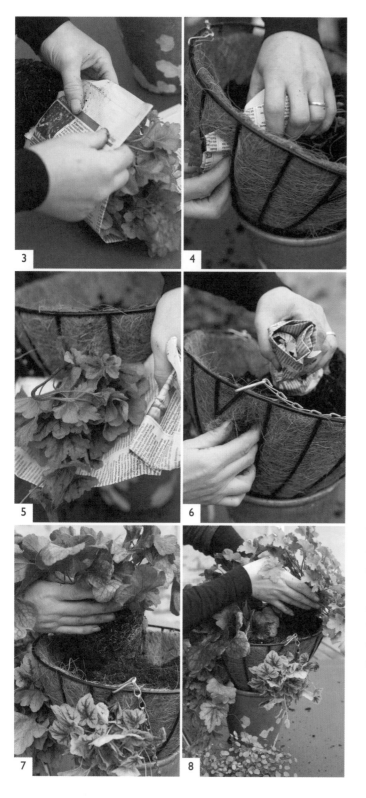

3 Soak the root balls of all the plants in water for at least 20 minutes. Take a heucherella plant out of its pot and carefully remove some of the potting compost to make the root ball smaller. This will allow more plants to be planted in the basket. Fold a sheet of newspaper into a strip approximately 8 x 12 in (20 x 30cm) and wrap it round the plant very carefully, enclosing the foliage.

4 Working slowly and gently, push the newspaper through the slit in the liner from the inside of the basket to the outside, foliage end first. Stop when all the leaves have been pushed through the liner.

5 Again working carefully to avoid damaging the plant, remove the newspaper and gently "fluff out" the leaves, making sure that none of them are squashed. Spread the roots out a little inside the basket.

6 Cut another two slits in the liner. There will be three slits in total so position them accordingly. Push two more heucherella plants through the slits in the same way as before.

7 Plant the remaining heucherella in the top of the basket, removing any excess potting compost from the root ball.

8 Plant the heuchera in the top of the basket in the same way, making sure that the surface of the root ball sits inside the basket and does not protrude.

9 Use the knife to cut three more slits in the liner between the heucherella plants, positioning the slits a little lower in the basket sides. Plant the muehlenbeckias, using the newspaper technique as before. These will help to hide the liner and basket.

10 Add the ivies to the basket, removing them from their pots and planting in the top of the basket, looking at the basket as a whole to find the best positions for them. Add a few handfuls of potting compost to the basket to fill it and make sure that the surface is even.

AFTERCARE

Hang the basket in its position and water thoroughly. Heucheras and heucherellas do not like to sit in very wet soil, so make sure that the basket is not overwatered. They are hardy and will withstand frosts, so your basket should look good all year round, although it will need feeding in the spring.

underplanting
an ornamental tree

This sweet little prunus tree with bare twiggy branches looks cute on its own, but underplanting it with senecio and cyclamen transforms it into a garden feature. Winding outdoor fairy lights around the branches gives it a frosty, twinkly look.

YOU WILL NEED

Small tree in a tub—this is a *Prunus incisa* 'Kojo-no-mai' (flowering cherry)

Gardening fork

Potting compost

7 x *Senecio cineraria* (silver ragwort)

4 x *Cyclamen persicum* (cyclamen)

Fairy lights suitable for outdoor use

1 Using the fork, dig over the soil around the tree, removing any weeds. Fork a few handfuls of potting compost into the top 4 in (10cm) of the soil. Soak the plants in water for 20 minutes to ensure the roots are moist. Plant the senecio around the edge of the tub.

2 Plant the cyclamen in the same way, in a ring inside the senecio. Firm the soil around the plants, adding a few handfuls of potting compost to fill any gaps. Wind the string of fairy lights around the bare branches.

AFTERCARE
Once the cyclamen are past their best, remove them and add other bedding plants. Or plant bulbs around the base of the prunus in late fall before adding the cyclamen and senecio, to give you blooms right through into spring.

ornamental *cabbages*

This fabulous container is proof, if it were needed, that winter gardens do not have to be dull. The vibrant tones of the ornamental cabbages, teamed with colorful heathers, will really brighten up a dull corner throughout the cold months of the year.

YOU WILL NEED

Galvanized tub

Crocks

Potting compost (ericaceous compost is recommended—although many heathers can tolerate alkaline compost, *Calluna vulgaris* will thrive only in ericaceous compost, so omit this plant if you have multi-purpose potting compost)

2 x *Brassica oleracea* (ornamental cabbage)

Artemisia 'Powis Castle' (mugwort)

Erica darleyensis 'Kramer's Red' (heather)

Calluna vulgaris 'Garden Girls' (heather)

Erica carnea 'Gracilis' (heather)

1 Make holes in the bottom of the tub if it does not have any (see page 26). Cover the holes with crocks so that they will not become blocked with potting compost.

2 Add potting compost to the tub, half filling it and smoothing it out evenly.

1

2

AFTERCARE

The tub will look after itself pretty well, but make sure the potting compost is moist, providing additional water if necessary. The tub should provide a burst of color throughout winter, provided it does not dry out too much. The cabbages can suffer slug damage, so check the undersides of the leaves and remove any slimy attackers.

3 Soak the root balls of all the plants in water for 20 minutes. Take the ornamental cabbages out of their pots and plant at the front of the tub, leaving a gap between them.

4 Plant the artemisia toward the back of the tub in the same way.

5 Take the heathers out of their pots and plant them around the cabbages and artemesia, arranging them so that they are evenly spread throughout the tub. Add more potting compost underneath the root balls if necessary, so that the tops of all the root balls are level with one another.

6 Add handfuls of potting compost to the tub, filling in any gaps and firming it all so that the plants are securely held in place.

Clematis and *pussy willow*

Choose a simple container to create a stylish display with sweet box, winter-flowering clematis, and pussy willow stems. Sweet box is an absolute must in the winter garden—it has a heavenly scent, so position it by the door. It is always a lovely surprise to discover the flowers on this clematis in the depths of winter.

YOU WILL NEED

Ceramic windowbox

Crocks

Potting compost

Sarcococca confusa (sweet box)

Clematis urophylla 'Winter Beauty' (winter-flowering clematis)

8 x *salix* (pussy willow) stems

Raffia

Bun moss

1 Put a few crocks over the drainage holes in the base of the windowbox to prevent them becoming blocked with potting compost.

2 Half-fill the box with potting compost, leveling it out evenly.

1

2

3 Soak the root balls of both plants in water for at least 20 minutes until they are soaking wet. Remove the pot from the sweet box and loosen the roots if necessary. Position it in the center of the container.

4 Remove the clematis from its pot and place to one side of the sweet box, planting it so that the surface of the root ball is a little deeper than the surface of the sweet box. Dig a little potting compost out from underneath if necessary. Fill around both plants with more compost, making sure the top of the clematis root ball is covered.

5 Put more potting compost into the windowbox to fill it and press around the plants to firm them in place.

6 Place four pussy willow stems at each end of the windowbox, pushing them right down to the bottom of the container.

AFTERCARE

Sweet box is a tough little plant and will put up with a fair amount of neglect. However, the clematis will require damp but not too wet potting compost, and will prefer a sheltered spot (a outside windowsill will be ideal). If the clematis gets very leggy, cut it back in spring after flowering and add fertilizer in the spring and summer.

7 Very carefully unfasten the clematis from its support pole and tie it to the pussy willow stems with raffia, making sure that it is securely held in place. Discard the support pole.

8 Gather the ends of the pussy willow stems together, overlapping them slightly, and tie them together with a length of raffia, finishing with a secure knot. Trim the raffia ends neatly. Cover the surface of the potting compost with pieces of bun moss, butting them up next to one another so that no compost is visible.

conifer *collection*

You may not have room for a collection of fully grown conifer trees in your garden, but a mini conifer patch is a very sweet addition. Choose plants in different shades and heights and plant in a tray, giving the roots space to grow outward. This metal tray even has carrying handles so that it can be moved around to act as a table decoration or container in different areas of your garden.

YOU WILL NEED

Metal tray

Hammer and nail

Crocks

Potting compost

Selection of small conifers—I used *Cupressus macrocarpa* 'Goldcrest' (Monterey cypress), *Cryptomeria japonica* 'Vilminiana' (Japanese cedar), *Chamaecyparis lawsoniana* 'Pembury Blue' (Lawson's cypress), *Cryptomeria japonica* 'Globosa Nana' (Japanese cedar), *Juniperus squamata* 'Blue Carpet' (flaky juniper), *Juniperus communis* 'Depressed Star' (common juniper), and *Cryptomeria japonica* 'Tilford Gold' (Japanese cedar)

1 Make drainage holes in the bottom of the tray if it does not have any. Use a hammer and nail and punch holes randomly all over the base.

2 Put a layer of crocks in the bottom of the tray, covering the drainage holes so that they will not become blocked with potting compost.

3 Scoop potting compost into the tray, half filling it and spreading the compost out evenly.

4 Soak the root balls of all the plants in water for about 20 minutes so they are all completely wet. Take the Monterey cypress out of its pot and tease the roots out a little if necessary. Plant it at the back of the tray, pushing it down into the potting compost slightly and making sure that it is vertical.

5 Remove the pot from the Japanese cedar 'Vilmoriniana' and plant next to the Monterey cypress in the same way. Make sure that the surfaces of the root balls are level.

6 Continue in the same way, planting the Lawson's cypress in front of the Monterey cypress.

7 Take the Japanese cedar 'Globosa Nana' from its pot and plant in the right-hand corner at the front of the tray.

8 Remove the flaky juniper from its pot and plant in the front left-hand corner. Squeeze in the two remaining conifers in the middle of the tray. Add more potting compost to fill in any gaps and level the surface, firming the compost down so that all the plants are held in place.

AFTERCARE

Water the tray and leave to drain. If the tray is in a sheltered spot where it will not receive any rainfall, water it regularly so that the potting compost remains moist, but be careful not to overwater. Stick your fingers in the potting compost to check the moisture—you will probably not be able to tell if the conifers are too dry by looking at them. Add fertilizer to the tray in the second year after planting to keep the conifers healthy.

chapter 2
beautiful bulbs

hyacinths in *glass jars*

I love the simplicity of these hyacinths, requiring just a bulb, glass jar, and water. They provide you with scented blooms in the middle of winter, and even before flowering they look beautiful, with their incredible roots twisting and weaving around the inside of the jar. Choose jars with narrow necks so the bulbs do not sit in water, varying the shapes and sizes of them to create an interesting display.

YOU WILL NEED

A selection of glass jars with narrow necks

Hyacinth bulbs suitable for forcing

Newspaper or scrap paper

1 Fill a clean glass jar with water, stopping just short of the rim. Dry around the rim to ensure that the bulb will not get wet.

2 Place a hyacinth bulb on the rim of the jar, with the pointed end facing upward. If the roots of the bulb have already started to sprout, tuck them into the jar, being careful not to damage them. If the bottom of the bulb does touch the water, remove the bulb and pour a little water out, as the bulb may start to rot if in direct contact with water.

3 To make a cover for the bulb, cut a piece of paper about 10 x 14 in (25 x 35cm). Fold it in half, matching up the two shorter sides.

4 With the fold along the top of the paper, fold the top right and left corners down to meet each other in the middle, then crease along the folds.

5 Fold the bottom edge of the top layer of paper up by about 1 in (2.5cm) and crease along the fold. Fold it over again by the same amount.

6 Repeat step 5 on the other side of the paper.

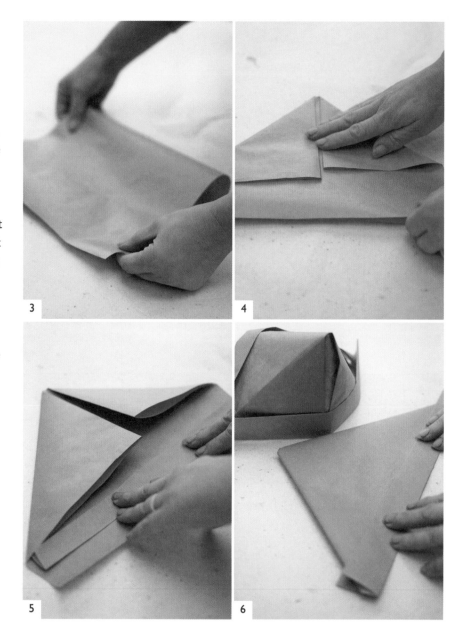

3

4

5

6

7 Open the hat shape up and carefully slip over the bulb and top of the jar, making sure that the bulb stays in place. Keep it in a dark, cool cupboard or shed.

8 Check the bulb after a few weeks, by which time the roots should have grown and the bulb should have started to shoot. If it has not, simply leave it for a little longer. When the bulb has started to grow, bring it out into the light and remove the paper cover. Leave in a warm spot and within a few weeks (depending on the conditions) the hyacinth should flower.

narcissi in *cream vases*

I have been collecting these old vases for several years and love the varied shapes and sizes of them. They look especially lovely grouped together, and in winter they make the perfect planters for indoor bulbs, forming bright and fragrant displays long before narcissi and daffodils start to appear out in the garden.

YOU WILL NEED

A selection of vases with large, open tops

Bulb fiber

Indoor narcissi bulbs ('Paper whites')

Pine cones or moss

1 Half-fill a vase with bulb fiber, pressing it down slightly to remove any air pockets. Place the bulbs on the bulb fiber, with the pointed ends of the bulbs facing upward, nestling them down in the bulb fiber. Plant several bulbs in each vase, leaving a small space between each.

2 Fill around the bulbs, leaving the tops sticking out of the bulb fiber. Water so the fiber is moist but not too wet, avoiding watering the bulbs directly. Place in a warm, light spot and water if the fiber becomes very dry. Bulbs should flower 6–8 weeks after planting. To hide the bulb fiber, add pine cones or moss around the shoots (wait until the shoots are a good height before adding, so their growth will not be stunted).

AFTERCARE

Check the bulb fiber regularly and water as necessary. The bulbs will not like very wet fiber so err on the side of caution, and as the vases do not have drainage holes, be careful not to overwater. After flowering, the bulbs can be planted in a sheltered spot outside, where they may flower again.

silver gray and *zingy lime*

Australian ivy is a lovely plant and perfect for container gardening. Its masses of delicate green leaves quiver gently in the wind, adding a graceful air to the urn and working as the perfect partner to the lime-green hyacinths that will soon bloom. Australian ivy is not hardy and prefers a sheltered spot, but should survive in low temperatures, simply losing a few leaves but still looking attractive.

1 Cover the drainage hole in the urn with a few crocks to prevent it becoming waterlogged. If the container you are using does not have any holes in the base, make some using a nail and hammer (see page 26).

2 Add potting compost to the urn, throwing in a few handfuls of gravel to help with drainage. Half-fill the urn with compost. Soak the muehlenbeckia in water for about 20 minutes to make sure that the root balls are moist.

YOU WILL NEED

Metal urn

Crocks

Potting compost

Gravel

7 x *Muehlenbeckia axillaris*
(creeping wire vine)

3 x *Hyacinthus orientalis*
(white hyacinth)

1

2

3 Remove the hyacinths from their pots and position them in the middle of the urn.

4 Take the muehlenbeckia out of their pots and place them around the hyacinth bulbs. You can leave a little gap around each plant, as they will quickly fill the space with their trailing stems and leaves.

5 Take a few handfuls of potting compost and fill in any gaps around the plants, firming the compost slightly to keep them all in place. Water the urn.

AFTERCARE

Check the potting compost regularly and, if it is very dry, water until moist. See page 64 for information on replanting the hyacinth bulbs after flowering.

potted *amaryllis*

Amaryllis are among the most showy of winter plants, with their huge, trumpet-like flowers and thick, chunky stems. The bulbs alone are things of beauty, with the sheer scale of them giving some indication of what is to follow. I love grouping them with ferns, moss, and bark for a spectacular display.

YOU WILL NEED

Amaryllis bulbs—I used 'Royal Red' and 'Rozetta'

Jar with a wide neck

Terra cotta pot 6–8 in (15–20cm) in diameter and at least twice the depth of the bulb

Crocks

Gravel

Grit or perlite

Potting compost

Saucer or bowl

1 Soak the roots of the bulbs in water overnight by filling a jar with tepid water and sitting the bulb on the jar. Make sure that only the roots are in the water and the bulb does not come in to contact with it.

2 Cover the drainage hole of the pot with a crock and add a layer of gravel to the bottom of the pot.

3 Add a handful of grit or perlite to the potting compost to lighten it and scoop some into the pot. The bulb needs to sit in the pot with the top part sticking above the surface of the compost mix, so add enough for this.

4 Place the bulb in the pot, being careful not to damage the roots. Add more potting compost around the bulb so that it is surrounded by it.

5 Place the pot on a saucer or in a bowl. Water the potting compost, trying not to pour water directly on to the bulb. Let the water drain off.

6 Place the pot in a warm, light spot, watering it regularly and making sure that it does not sit in water. The bulb should start to sprout straight away, and keeping it warm will help speed up the blooms.

AFTERCARE

Keep the potting compost moist and display in a cool place when flowering to prolong the blooms. Once the bulb has flowered, feed the pot with liquid fertilizer, leave in a greenhouse or sheltered spot outside over the summer, and keep watered. Cut the leaves back to about 4 in (10cm) in early fall, either re-pot or replace the top half of the potting compost, and grow again, ready to flower again in the winter.

bulbs in *metal molds*

Bulbs signal the start of spring, but forcing bulbs indoors will furnish you with color and scent a little earlier. Adding moss around the bulbs will hide the potting compost.

YOU WILL NEED

Old metal jello or blancmange molds

Crocks

Gravel

Bulb fiber or potting compost

Hyacinthus orientalis (hyacinth)

Muscari armeniacum (grape hyacinth)

Crocus x *cultorum* 'Jeanne d'Arc' (crocus)

Moss (available from florists)

1 If your container does not have drainage holes, use bulb fiber that regulates moisture. If your container does have holes, add crocks and a ¾ in (1.5cm) layer of gravel or grit. For hyacinths, half-fill the container with potting compost or bulb fiber. For smaller bulbs, fill the container.

2 Place the hyacinths on the potting compost and add more compost or fiber, leaving the top of each bulb sticking out. For smaller bulbs, push the bulbs down (pointed ends facing up) so the tips are below the surface (crocus about 4 in/10cm below the surface and grape hyacinth about 2 in/5cm).

3 Water, but do not saturate, the bulb fiber. Store in a cool, dark place for about 12 weeks, checking occasionally to ensure they are not too dry. When the tips are about 1 in (2.5cm) high, bring into daylight. Add moss to hide the compost or fiber.

AFTERCARE

Keep the potting compost or bulb fiber moist but not too wet. Display in a light, draft-free place. To get the bulbs to bloom for a specific date, water a little more and keep them in a warm place to speed up the process.

china tureen of *snowdrops*

Snowdrops are always a welcome sight in a winter garden, their delicate little white flower heads emerging through the bare soil when there is very little else around, marking the start of a new growing season. Planting a few bulbs indoors in fall will provide you with flowers several weeks before their outdoor partners.

YOU WILL NEED

China tureen

Gravel or grit

Potting compost

Galanthus nivalis (snowdrop bulbs)

Moss or decorative grit

1 Add a few handfuls of gravel or grit to the tureen. Put a few scoops of potting compost in the tureen, mixing the gravel or grit into it. Fill to about 2 in (5cm) from the rim.

2 Place the bulbs on the surface of the potting compost, spacing about 2 in (5cm) apart, with the slightly pointed end facing upward.

3 Cover the bulbs with potting compost, filling the tureen up to the rim. Add moss or decorative grit to the surface of the compost when the bulbs have started to grow.

AFTERCARE

Water the potting compost carefully so that it is moist but not too wet. Keep the tureen in a cool place and check the compost regularly, adding a little water if it gets too dry. Do not let it dry out completely, as this may stop the bulbs growing. After flowering, the bulbs can be re-potted and kept in a cool, dark place, ready to flower again next year.

signs of *spring*

All the plants in this wooden crate are most definitely winter plants, but with their vibrant lime-green colors and bright white flowers they bring a springlike freshness to the winter garden. I used forced bulbs in this container, but you could plant bulbs in the fall and they will flower toward the end of winter.

YOU WILL NEED

Wooden crate

Thick black plastic

Staple gun

Potting compost

Gravel

Dryopteris filix-mas (male fern)

Heuchera 'Lime Marmalade'

Helleborus niger 'Verboom Beauty' (hellebore)

Narcissus (daffodils)

Tulipa 'Coquette' (tulip)

1 Line the wooden crate with plastic to keep the potting compost in place and to help protect the crate. Staple the plastic to the inside of the crate, folding it at the corners and stopping it just short of the top of the crate so that it will not be seen.

2 Make a few small holes in the bottom of the plastic for drainage. Add a bottom layer of potting compost mixed with several shovels of gravel, then half-fill the crate with just potting compost.

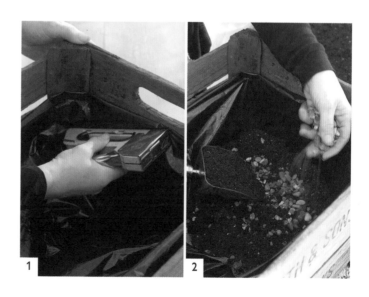

3 Soak the root balls of the fern, heuchera, and hellebore (the bulbs will not need soaking). Take the fern from its pot and plant it in the crate, positioning it at one of the back corners.

4 Remove the heuchera from its pot and place it in the crate, fluffing up the leaves over the edge of the crate.

5 Remove the hellebore from its pot and plant it toward the front of the crate.

6 Remove the narcissi from their pots and dot them around in the crate, adding more potting compost to hold them in place.

7 Plant the tulips, taking them from their pots and filling in any gaps with them. Add handfuls of potting compost to fill any holes and level the surface of the compost to keep the plants in place.

AFTERCARE

Water the crate and leave to drain. The bulbs will flower for a couple of weeks if the crate is kept outside.

To keep it looking good thoughout winter, simply add new bulbs, removing the ones that have flowered and planting them in a light, sheltered spot in the garden, to flower again next year.

chapter 3
winter color

an abundance of *berries*

Plants grow very little during winter, which means you can combine lots in a tub, filling it with as many berries and as much color and foliage as you can, creating an abundant look without worrying that the plants will be short of room. When the plants reach their growing season and get bigger, it may be worth moving some to other containers, but for the first winter they can be enjoyed en masse.

YOU WILL NEED

Galvanized tub or bucket

Broken bricks or large crocks

Potting compost

2 x *Pyracantha* (firethorn)

4 x *Solanum pseudocapsicum* (winter cherry)

4 x *Sedum spathulifolium* 'Purpureum' (purple stonecrop)

1 Make sure that the base of the tub has a few drainage holes. If not, make some using a drill and bit suitable for metal, or if the metal is thin enough, a hammer and large nail. Create large holes to allow ample drainage. Cover the base of the tub with crocks or broken bricks to help with drainage, then pour potting compost into the tub, filling it about three-quarters full.

2 Soak the root balls of all the plants in water for at least 20 minutes (or longer, if necessary, for the larger ones) so that the roots are wet. Take the largest pyracantha out of its pot, and tease the roots slightly to encourage them to grow outward. Place it at the back of the tub. Add more potting compost to hold the plant in place and to raise the surface level if the remaining plants have smaller root balls.

3 Take the smaller pyracantha out of its pot, loosening the roots a little as before. Place it in the tub, turning it so that its good side faces forward. Add more potting compost around it to hold it in place.

4 Take the solanum out of their pots and dot them around the front of the tub, checking to see that the arrangement looks good before planting them.

5 Remove the sedum from their pots and plant them toward the front of the tub, filling in the gaps between the solanum. Add handfuls of potting compost to fill in any holes, although the tub will probably be fairly full by now.

6 Remove any stakes and canes from the plants so that they spill out a little and look more natural. Water well and leave to drain.

AFTERCARE

The tub should not require additional watering, unless it is in a particularly sheltered spot. Check it from time to time and if it is very dry, water.

windowbox *pansies*

This lovely old container makes a charming windowbox, planted up with richly colored pansies that will grow happily in shallow potting compost. Adding small-scale ferns creates more interest, with bun moss (which I love so much I could use in every container!) disguising the compost and helping to keep moisture in.

YOU WILL NEED

Metal windowbox or similar

Hammer and large nail

Gravel

Potting compost

Selection of *viola* x *wittrockiana* (pansy)—I used 8 plants

2 x *Dryopteris erythrosora* 'Prolifica' (lacy autumn fern)

Bun moss (available from floristry suppliers)

1 The windowbox will require drainage holes, so if the one you are using does not have any, hammer a nail through the metal at intervals along its length.

2 Add gravel to the bottom of the windowbox, covering the base all the way along and spreading it out evenly. This will prevent the container becoming waterlogged.

3 Scoop the potting compost into the windowbox, half-filling it. Press it down slightly to form an even layer.

4 Soak the pansies and ferns in water for about 20 minutes to make sure that the roots are wet. Take a pansy out of its pot or tray and position at one end of the windowbox.

5 Continue to plant pansies along the windowbox, placing them quite close together.

6 Take the ferns from their pots, loosening their roots slightly to encourage them to grow out into the windowbox. Plant them between some of the pansies.

7 Add more potting compost around the plants, and firm them in so that they are securely held in place. Take pieces of moss and lay them around the plants so that none of the compost shows.

AFTERCARE

Water the windowbox and allow to drain. Keep the compost moist but not too wet, checking it regularly and watering when necessary. Windowboxes can often fall under the shelter of the house and not get much rainwater, so additional watering may be necessary. Deadheading the pansies regularly will encourage them to keep flowering throughout winter.

winter *blues*

I love the color of this old enamel tub, but have no idea what its original use was. I presume it came from a farm, but now it is employed as an attractive planter with soft, frosty-looking foliage plants and striking pink cyclamen to add a punch.

YOU WILL NEED

Large container

Crocks

Potting compost

Euphorbia characias 'Glacial Blue' (spurge)

Eucalyptus gunii (cider gum tree)

Convolvulus cneorum (convolvulus)

Festuca glauca 'Intense Blue' (blue fescue)

2 x *Cyclamen persicum* (cyclamen)

Variegated *Hedera helix* (ivy)

1 Cover the drainage holes in the bottom of the container with a few crocks. If the tub has a solid base, you will need to make some holes using a hammer and nail (see page 90).

2 This churn-style container is quite deep and would require a large quantity of potting compost to fill it, so adding a few broken bricks or stones or similar to the bottom reduces the amount of compost required. It will also help with drainage, preventing the compost becoming waterlogged. Blocks of polystyrene also act as an effective filler.

3 Add the potting compost to the container, filling it about two-thirds full. Press the compost down slightly to make sure that there are no air pockets, then level the surface of the compost with your hands.

4 Soak all the root balls of the plants in water for about 20 minutes to make sure that they are completely wet. Take the euphorbia from its pot, tease the roots slightly if necessary to encourage them to grow out, and place in the container, pressing it up against the side.

5 Plant the convolvulus by placing it in the container next to the euphorbia. Ensure that the surface of the plant's soil is level with that of the other plants in the container.

6 Remove the eucalyptus from its pot and plant in the same way, making sure that it stands upright against the side of the container.

7 The festuca has been divided into two plants so that two smaller clumps can be planted on each side of the container. To do this, hold the plant in both hands and dig your thumbs into the middle of the plant, then pull apart to rip in to two. Plant the clumps in the container.

8 Remove the cyclamen from their pots and squeeze them into the front of the container, being careful not to damage the flowers.

9 Take the ivy from its pot and plant at the front of the container so that it trails down the outside.

10 Add more potting compost to the container to fill in any gaps around the plants, and level off the surface.

glass jar *terrarium*

Terrariums are a lovely means of creating small gardens inside the house, and are often used to grow succulents and ferns. Planting flowering plants in an open-topped glass jar creates a pretty indoor garden that will bring color and beauty into your home.

YOU WILL NEED

Large glass jar with a wide neck

Gravel

Ground charcoal (pet stores should stock this)

Potting compost

Scoop

Helleborus niger (choose an alpine variety with a small root ball)

Viola x *wittrockiana* (pansy)

Humata tyermanii (bunny fern)

Moss (available from florists)

Soft paintbrush

1 Clean and dry the jar thoroughly before you start. Carefully place a layer of gravel in the bottom of the jar (adding it in handfuls rather than pouring it in, so that it does not shatter the glass). The gravel should be about ¾ in (2cm) thick and evenly spread over the bottom of the jar.

2 Sprinkle charcoal powder over the gravel, completely covering it. This will help to absorb odors from the potting compost, ensuring that the terrarium does not smell.

3

4

5

6

3 Check that the potting compost is damp before using—water it if necessary, letting it drain slightly before using it. Add the potting compost to the jar, making a layer about 2 in (5cm) thick. Add it using a small scoop or your hand rather than pouring it in, so that it does not make too much mess inside the jar.

4 Take the hellebore out of its pot and carefully remove any excess soil from around the roots. Make a shallow dip in the potting compost inside the jar and place the hellebore in it, spreading the roots out a little and anchoring it in place with a little more potting compost if necessary, so that it sits firmly upright.

5 Take the pansy from its pot and plant in the jar in the same way, placing it toward the back of the jar, next to the hellebore.

6 Add the fern, again removing excess soil from the roots, and plant toward the front of the jar, adding more potting compost if necessary. Firm around all three plants so that they sit firmly in the compost.

7 Tear the sheet of moss into pieces and place them on the surface of the potting compost, around the plants. Make sure that all the potting compost is covered, adding smaller pieces of moss if necessary.

8 Using the soft paintbrush, clean up the inside of the jar and brush any bits of potting compost from the leaves and flowers to tidy them up.

AFTERCARE

Make sure that the potting compost remains moist but not too wet (stick your finger into the compost to check), watering sparely when necessary. Keep the terrarium indoors in a light spot and deadhead the pansy regularly. With the right conditions, the plants should keep flowering for several weeks or even months, but the foliage will look lovely too.

winter *whites*

The combination of a dwarf spruce, the red berries of skimmia, and the pretty white pansies has a beautifully fresh wintry look. The old enamel tub was a flea-market find that is the perfect size for these plants and would look lovely placed by the front door.

YOU WILL NEED

White enamel tub

Crocks

Ericaceous potting compost

Skimmia reevesiana (skimmia)

Picea glauca conica (dwarf spruce)

4 x *Viola* (viola)

Moss (available from florists)

1 The tub used here already had drainage holes in the bottom but if yours doesn't, then add a few using a large nail and a hammer, making the holes as large as you can (see page 90). Cover the holes with crocks so that they will not get blocked with potting compost. Add the potting compost, spreading it out evenly in the tub and filling it about a third full.

2 Soak the plants in water for about 20 minutes (the larger plants may need a little longer if the potting compost has dried out). Remove the spruce from its pot and carefully pull the roots to loosen them a little—this will encourage them to spread. Place the spruce toward the back of the tub.

3 Plant the skimmia next to the spruce. Take the pansies out of their trays and plant them along the front of the tub. Press the potting compost to firm it and keep the plants in place. Add pieces of moss around the plants if there is a lot of compost showing, although this can be omitted if you wish as the plants will eventually cover the surface of the compost as they grow.

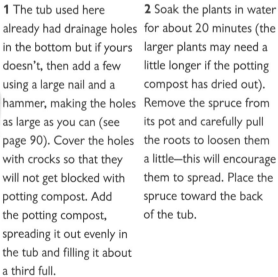

AFTERCARE

The skimmia will happily grow in a container and this variety does not require male and female plants to be grown together to produce berries, unlike other varieties. Skimmia and dwarf spruces prefer slightly acidic soil and will be better in ericaceous potting compost. If this is not available, they will be fine in ordinary potting compost over the winter but may need to be replanted the following spring.

vibrant *cyclamen*

Cyclamen are a welcome addition to the winter garden, adding shots of scarlet, bright fuchsia, and pale pink to the dark and gloomy days. Garden centers often stock them in a range of colors, and grouping together several plants in different shades can create a focal point in the garden, especially if you add trailing ivy to link them together. Here an old kitchen pan stand gives the plants height, creating a vertical display in a corner of the garden.

YOU WILL NEED

Collection of old cake tins or pans

Nail

Hammer

Crocks

Potting compost

Gravel

Cyclamen persicum (cyclamen)

Hedera helix (ivy)

1 Make holes in the bottom of the cake tins to help with drainage, using a hammer and nail. Dot the holes around the base, making at least six in each tin.

2 Place a few crocks over the holes to prevent them becoming clogged with potting compost.

3 Add the potting compost and a few handfuls of gravel to the cake tin, half-filling it and spreading the compost out evenly.

4 Soak the cyclamen and ivy in water for about 20 minutes to make sure that the root balls are completely wet. Take the cyclamen out of its pot and loosen the root ball slightly, being careful not to disturb the roots too much. Position it in the tin. If adding ivy as well, take it out of its pot and place it in the tin, too.

5 Add more potting compost around the plant and firm down so the plants are held securely in place. Repeat this for the remaining cake tins using the cyclamen and ivy.

AFTERCARE

Keep the potting compost moist but not too wet, otherwise the cyclamen may become quite slimy and will not flower. Deadhead the cyclamen regularly to keep them blooming.

shades of *pink and green*

This metal box was a real find in a secondhand market, and planting it with subtle, muted colors creates a sophisticated display. Hellebores are such beautiful plants and come in an array of stunning colors. This one, with its flowers in dusky pink and pale cream, looks stunning for several months.

YOU WILL NEED

Container

Hammer and large nail

Crocks

Potting compost

Helleborus x *ballardiae* or x *ericsmithii* 'Maestro' (hellebore)

Euphorbia 'Despina'

Woodwardia unigemmata (walking fern)

Hebe 'Heartbreaker' (veronica)

Leucothoe scarletta (dog hobble)

Hedera helix (ivy)

1 If the container you are using does not have drainage holes, make some all over its base using a hammer and nail (or a drill and appropriate drill bit if it is very solid).

2 Add crocks to the base of the box, covering the holes to help prevent the potting compost becoming too waterlogged and not draining well when watered.

3 Shovel potting compost into the box, half-filling it. Spread the compost out evenly, making sure that there are no air pockets.

4 Soak the root balls of all the plants in water for at least 20 minutes and make sure that they are thoroughly wet. Take the hellebore out of its pot and tease the roots out a little to encourage them to spread. Place it toward the back of the box and secure around it with a little potting compost to hold it in place.

5 Remove the euphorbia from its pot, pull gently at the roots, as before, being careful not to damage them, and put it in the box next to the hellebore. Anchor it with a few handfuls of potting compost.

6 Take the fern out of its pot, gently pull at the roots a little if necessary (if it is very pot bound), and plant it next to the euphorbia in the box.

7 Plant the hebe at the front of the box, again pulling at the roots if necessary and securing with a handful or two of potting compost.

9 Adding an ivy plant to the front of the box will soften the look a little and create more interest. Plant it in the same way as before, tucking it into the front corner and draping the trailing stems over the front of the box. Add more potting compost all round the plants and firm the surface to level it all.

8 Place the leucothoe in the front of the box, removing its pot and planting as before.

AFTERCARE

Water the box and leave to drain. The box will require additional watering only in very dry periods, and the plants will look after themselves over the winter.

poinsettia *pots*

On their own, poinsettias can look a little insignificant, but grouping several together in simple cream planters creates a beautiful display that is a real show-stopper.

YOU WILL NEED

Pots

Crocks

Rough sand or grit

Potting compost

Euphorbia pulcherrima
(poinsettias)

1 Place a crock in the base of the pot to cover the hole. To aid drainage, mix sand or grit into the potting compost, using one part sand or grit to three parts compost. Put some of this mix in the pot, bearing in mind the size of the root ball.

2 Place the poinsettia in the pot, with the surface of the plant's soil just below the pot's rim. Add more compost mixture below it if necessary and fill around the plant so it is held in place. Flatten the surface. Water the pot and let the water drain off.

AFTERCARE

Check the potting compost regularly and water only when the top feels dry. Aim to keep it constantly just moist rather than flooding with water every now and then. Feed monthly with liquid fertilizer mixed with water (follow manufacturer's instructions) to keep it blooming. In a light spot, away from drafts, it should reward you well for several months.

frosty *windowbox*

Choosing plants in pale greens and whites creates a charming windowbox that will look good throughout the winter. Cushion bush has a lovely frosty look to it and is evergreen but can tolerate only light frosts, so if you live in a cold area it may be worth replacing it with santolinas or other similarly whitish-green foliage plants.

YOU WILL NEED

Painted wooden windowbox with holes in the base

Crocks

Potting compost

Dorycnium hirsutus 'Little Boy Blue' (hairy canary clover)

Convolvulus cneorum (convolvulus)

Artemisia 'Powis Castle' (mugwort)

2 x *Cyclamen persicum* (cyclamen)

2 x *Calocephalus brownii* (cushion bush)

1 Soak the plants in water for 20 minutes until the root balls are completely wet. Cover the base of the box with crocks, then half-fill with potting compost and level it. Plant the clover in the back left corner, convolvulus in the middle, and the mugwort in the back right corner.

2 Plant the cushion bush in the front corners of the box and two cyclamen in the remaining space at the front. Add more potting compost around the plants, holding the leaves back so you can fill any gaps. Firm the potting compost down around the plants, and water.

1

2

AFTERCARE

Keep the potting compost moist but not too wet and check it regularly, especially if it will not catch any rainwater. Deadhead the cyclamen regularly.

black and *gold*

This striking black pot is complemented well by plants in bold colors. The golden green of the pittosporum contrasts well with the yellow salix, black grasses, and lime-green heuchera to give an unusual winter container with a contemporary feel.

YOU WILL NEED

Large black pot

Large crocks

Polystyrene

Potting compost

Salix alba 'Golden Ness' (golden willow)

Pittosporum tenuifolium 'Warnham Gold' (New Zealand pittosporum)

Heuchera 'Lime Marmalade' (coral bells)

Carex comans 'Bronze' (New Zealand hair grass)

Ophiopogon planiscapus 'Nigrescens' (black mondo)

Raffia

1 Cover the drainage hole in the bottom of the pot with a few large crocks to help with drainage. As this pot is so deep, adding broken pieces of polystyrene to the bottom of it will reduce the amount of potting compost needed and will also help to insulate the pot.

2 Add potting compost, making sure that there are no air pockets around the polystyrene pieces. Fill the pot about three-quarters full.

3   4   5

3 Soak the root balls of all the plants in water for about 20 minutes until they are completely soaked through. Take the willow from its pot and plant in the center of the pot, adding or removing compost from underneath it so that the surface of its soil is about 2 in (5cm) below the rim of the pot.

4 Remove the pittosporum from its pot and plant it behind and level with the willow in the same way.

5 Take the heuchera from its pot and plant it in front of the willow, firming it in place and draping the leaves over the edge of the pot.

6 Take the carex from its pot and tuck it into the pot so that the fronds drape over the edge.

6

7 Plant the ophiopogon at the edge of the pot, teasing out the roots gently with your fingers if necessary. Add more potting compost to the pot if necessary and level the surface.

8 For a quirky finish, tie the willow branches together with a length of raffia, finishing with a secure knot. Undo the ties when the plant starts to bud.

AFTERCARE

Water the pot and leave in a spot where it will catch rainfall. Check the potting compost every now and then to make sure it is damp, but all the plants are quite hardy and will not require much tending.

enamel tub *tower*

This display is very easy to make, and is a lovely way to make a real feature of simple winter plants. I used old enamel tubs, but terra cotta or ceramic pots in different sizes would work as well—just ensure they are stable when planted. Add more bedding plants to replace the narcissi and pansies as they go over.

YOU WILL NEED

Three enamel pots in different sizes

Hammer and nail

Two plant pots

Crocks

Potting compost with sand or grit added for drainage

3 x *Erica cinerea* f. *aureifolia* 'Windlebrooke' (bell heather)

6 x *Viola* 'Red Blotch' (pansy)

6 x *Viola* 'Raspberry' (pansy)

3 x *Hedera helix* (ivy)

3 x *Muehlenbeckia axillaris* (creeping wire vine)

Pteris ensiformis 'Evergemiensis' (silver lace fern)

Narcissi

Primula (primrose)

1 The enamel tubs will need drainage holes in the bottom, so if your tubs do not have any, make several randomly around the edge of each tub using a hammer and nail (or a drill and suitable bit if the tubs are very thick).

2 Place one of the small plant pots upturned in the center of the largest enamel tub. Put crocks over the drainage holes of the tub so that they will not become blocked with potting compost.

1

2

3 Fill the tub with potting compost, making sure that the upturned pot stays in the center of the tub and the compost is level with the base of the upturned pot. Press the compost down firmly, adding more if the surface drops a little.

4 Put the medium tub on top of this, moving it slightly to one side while you plant the tub. The upturned plant pot will support it and prevent it sinking down into the potting compost.

5 Soak the root balls of all the plants in water for a while so that the compost is wet. Remove the pots from some of the plants and plant them around the rim of the bottom tub, then move the second tub back into the middle and continue to plant round the edge.

6 Repeat this method with the second tub, placing an upturned pot in the center as before, adding crocks, and then filling with potting compost. Place the smallest tub on top.

7 Plant around the edge again, moving the tub slightly to make it easier to plant if necessary.

8 Put crocks in the base of the top tub and fill the tub with potting compost. Plant narcissi in the top tub, firming the compost to hold the plants in place so they stand upright.

9 Add ivy to the top tub and arrange it so that it drapes down the tiers. Finish with a few pansy plants.

AFTERCARE

Water each layer of the tub. Keep an eye on the potting compost. Do not let it dry out completely, but check to make sure the bottom layer especially does not become waterlogged (as the water drains down through the tower to the bottom). Deadhead the pansies to keep them blooming throughout winter. Add spring bedding plants when the winter plants start to go over and the arrangement will look good throughout the seasons. Use a liquid fertilizer every few weeks from late spring onward to keep the plants looking their best.

garden gate *welcome*

Holly and berries shout out "winter," and here they are combined with heather and ivy to make a handsome container that will require little attention. The plump red berries add a splash of color, accentuated by the simple cream planter.

1 This container is studded with holes, which look lovely and provide good drainage. To prevent the potting compost falling out, line the container with moss. Press sheets of moss around the inside of the planter, then half-fill the planter with potting compost, making sure there are no air pockets and pressing the compost against the moss to keep it in place.

2 Soak the plants in water for 20 minutes so the root balls are wet. Carefully remove the prickly heath from its pot (the stems are spiny), loosen the roots if necessary, and place in the planter. Loosen the holly roots if necessary, and plant next to the prickly heath, adding more potting compost so the root balls are level. Plant the heather and ivy in the same way. Add a few handfuls of potting compost to fill in any gaps, then water.

YOU WILL NEED

Large planter

Moss (available from florists)

Potting compost, with a few scoops of gravel added for drainage

Pernettya mucronata (prickly heath)

Ilex aquifolium 'Argentea Marginata' (holly)

Erica darleyensis 'Kramer's Red' (heather)

Hedera helix (ivy)

AFTERCARE

The pot will probably not require additional watering over winter, although if it is situated in a sheltered spot, check the potting compost occasionally and water if very dry.

chapter 4
winter harvest

swiss chard and *sorrel*

Swiss chard is a lovely winter crop—plant it with evergreen salad burnet, red-veined sorrel, and pansies to create a pretty and practical winter planter. Sow seeds in late summer or early fall and the chard will be ready to harvest in winter.

YOU WILL NEED

Seed tray

Potting compost

Beta vulgaris (Swiss chard) seeds

Enamel dish

Crocks

Gravel

Sanguisorba minor (salad burnet)

Rumex sanguineus (sorrel)

Viola x *wittrockiana* (pansies)

1 Fill a seed tray with potting compost, ideally sieving it to ensure there are no lumps. Sow seeds about 3–4 in (7.5–10cm) apart and cover with a little more compost. Water and leave in a warm, draft-free spot. Check the potting compost every few days and water sparingly if necessary.

2 When the seedlings have 5 or 6 small leaves, they are ready to transplant. Cover the drainage holes of the dish with crocks and add potting compost with a few handfuls of gravel in the bottom layer. Make a hole in the compost and place the roots of a few seedlings in the hole, with the lower leaves just above the surface. Gently firm in.

3 Soak the salad burnet and sorrel plants in water for 10 minutes. Plant around the Swiss chard seedlings, with pansies in between. Water the container and leave in a warm spot.

windowbox of *herbs*

A simple windowbox filled with hardy herbs is essential for the cook during the winter months. Display it on a kitchen windowsill so you always have fresh herbs to hand. Planting a senecio and a few narcissi adds more interest to the windowbox and creates a more decorative display. Lift the narcissi bulbs after flowering and plant them in a sheltered spot in the garden, where they should flower the following year.

YOU WILL NEED

Ceramic windowbox

Crocks

Potting compost

Rosmarinus officinalis (rosemary)

Salvia officinalis (sage)

Laurus nobilis (bay)

Senecio cineraria (silver ragwort)

2 x narcissi

1 Cover the drainage holes in the bottom of the windowbox with a few crocks so that they do not become blocked with potting compost.

2 Scoop potting compost into the windowbox, filling it about half full. Level the surface.

3 Soak the root balls of all the plants (apart from the narcissi) in water for about 20 minutes. Remove the pot from the rosemary, loosening the roots with your fingers if it is pot bound. Place in the windowbox, pushing it down slightly so that it sits upright.

4 Take the sage from its pot and plant in the windowbox in the same way.

5 Plant the bay and the senecio in the windowbox, again pushing them down so that the surface of the root balls is about 1 in (2.5cm) below the rim of the box.

6 Add a little more potting compost around the plants to hold them firmly in place.

7 Take the narcissi from their pots, dig a hole in the potting compost behind the herbs with your hand, and carefully plant them in the windowbox, pushing them down into the potting compost so they stand upright. Firm the potting compost around them.

AFTERCARE

Water the windowbox and keep the potting compost moist but not too wet. The herbs can all be picked and eaten over winter, but they will not grow very much so be careful not to over-pick them. Remove the narcissi once they have flowered, deadheading them and planting them out in the garden. Once the herbs start to grow in spring, the windowbox will fill out well.

edible cabbages
and herbs

These cabbages not only taste delicious, but also look stunning. Sow seeds in late summer so the cabbages have a chance to get going before winter, or buy small cabbage plants and plant straight into your container.

1

1 Fill the seed tray with potting compost, ideally sieving it to get rid of any lumps, and level the surface. Sprinkle cabbage seeds on the surface of the compost, making sure they are at least ⅜ in (1cm) apart. Cover with a little more compost and water. Leave the tray in a warm, sheltered spot and make sure the compost is kept damp but not too wet,. The seedlings should appear after 7–10 days.

2 When the seedlings have 5 or 6 leaves, they are ready to transplant. Cover the drainage holes in the tub with crocks, then fill it with potting compost, adding a few handfuls of gravel to the bottom layer to aid drainage. Make a hole in the compost, carefully take a few seedlings from the tray, and drop the roots into the hole. Pour water into the hole and gently press the compost around the seedlings to hold them in place.

2

3 Soak the sage and thyme plants in water for at least 10 minutes, then plant them around the seedlings, leaving enough room for the cabbages to grow. Water the container and leave to drain.

3

YOU WILL NEED

Seed tray

Potting compost

Cabbage seeds

Galvanized tub

Crocks

Gravel

Salvia officinalis 'Purpurascens' (purple sage)

Thymus serpyllum (thyme)

AFTERCARE

Keep in a warm spot and water when necessary. The cabbages are hardy and will be fine in cold weather. Either harvest whole cabbages or pick leaves to eat, leaving the plants in situ.

evergreen *bay tree*

Bay trees are always a lovely addition to the garden, and work well by front doors and gates. Planted in a large terra cotta planter, this bay tree is complemented by narcissi, iris, primula, and ivy, which form the underplanting, with decorative twigs added for more interest and to act as a support for the flowers.

YOU WILL NEED

Large terracotta pot

Bubble wrap

Crocks

Potting compost, with a couple of shovels of grit added to improve drainage

Laurus nobilis (bay tree)

2 x variegated *Hedera helix* (ivy)

8 x *Primula* (primroses)

Iris reticulata 'Alida' (mini iris)

Narcissi bulbs

Twigs

1 Wrap bubble wrap around the inside of the pot, but don't cover the base. This will help to insulate the pot. Cover the drainage hole with a few crocks.

2 Soak the root balls of the plants in water for at least 20 minutes (the tree may need longer to ensure it is completely wet). Half-fill the pot with potting compost. Plant the tree in the center of the pot, spreading the roots out as much as possible. Make sure the surface of the tree's soil is about 2 in (5cm) below the pot's rim. Add or remove compost as necessary.

3 Fill the pot with more potting compost up to the same level, firming it so that the bay tree sits vertically in the pot without wobbling. Check that the trunk is not at an angle and move the plant to straighten it if necessary.

4 Take the ivy plants from their pots. Dig a hole in the potting compost at both front corners of the pot and plant the ivy, firming the potting compost around them to hold them in place.

5 Plant the primulas around the pot, leaving gaps for the iris and narcissi, and firm the compost around them. Be careful not to get potting compost on the flowers, and handle them gently as the blooms are quite delicate.

6 Plant the iris and narcissi randomly around the pot, planting the narcissi quite deep so that they will be less likely to flop over. Add additional potting compost to fill in any gaps if necessary. Push twigs randomly into the compost to add a decorative detail and to prop up the narcissi if necessary.

AFTERCARE

Keep the potting compost moist but not too wet, as overwatering may cause the roots to rot. Bay trees are happy in cold weather, but if your container is in a very open spot, it may be worth covering it in horticultural fleece during long spells of very cold weather. The bay tree will live happily in a pot longterm, but add fertilizer tablets to the pot from spring through late fall and re-pot after a couple of years. Terra cotta pots are beautiful but may need additional care over winter as they can easily suffer frost damage. Lining the pot with bubble wrap or polystyrene will help, and it is a good idea to wrap the outside of the pot during very cold or frosty spells

winter *lettuce*

Picking home-grown lettuce is a real treat over winter, and it will crop for several months. It is very easy to grow if you provide shelter and cover when the weather hits very low temperatures. When buying seeds, make sure you select a variety suitable for winter growing.

YOU WILL NEED

Container with tiers

Black plastic bags or sacks

Staple gun

Potting compost

Lettuce seeds, suitable for growing in winter

Water sprayer

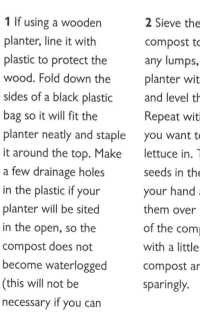

1 If using a wooden planter, line it with plastic to protect the wood. Fold down the sides of a black plastic bag so it will fit the planter neatly and staple it around the top. Make a few drainage holes in the plastic if your planter will be sited in the open, so the compost does not become waterlogged (this will not be necessary if you can control the watering).

2 Sieve the potting compost to get rid of any lumps, then fill the planter with compost and level the surface. Repeat with the tiers you want to grow lettuce in. Take the seeds in the palm of your hand and sprinkle them over the surface of the compost. Cover with a little more compost and water sparingly.

3 The seedlings should start to grow after about a week. Water them with a sprayer rather than a watering can, which can be a little harsh and can flatten the seedlings.

AFTERCARE

As the seedlings start to sprout, thin them out (by pulling up some of the plants) to give them more room to grow. The plants that you pull out can be added to salads so need not be wasted. Winter lettuce will need a very sheltered spot (a glasshouse is ideal), but covering the container with horticultural fleece or plastic in very cold weather will ensure that the plants continue to grow.

index

resources

UNITED KINGDOM

Alexandra Nurseries
Estate House
56B Parish Lane
London SE20 7LJ
020 8778 4145
www.alexandranurseries.co.uk
A lovely range of plants and vintage
containers and pots.

Anthropologie
00800 0026 8476
www.anthropologie.eu
Interesting tubs and containers
suitable for gardening.

Apta Pots
01233 621090 for stockists
www.apta.co.uk
A huge selection of ceramic, terra
cotta, and stone pots available from
garden centres around the country.

Crocus
01344 578000
www.crocus.co.uk
Large selection of plants and
gardening equipment available by
mail order.

Heucheraholics
01590 670581
www.heucheraholics.co.uk
A must for heuchera, heucherella,
and tiarella lovers. A wide range
of good-quality plants available by
mail order.

Mabel and Rose
01993 878861
www.mabelandrose.com
Mail-order company stocking
beautiful old containers, tubs, and
pots, as well as vintage gardening
equipment.

Petersham Nurseries
Church Lane (off Petersham Road)
Richmond
Surrey TW10 7AB
020 8940 5230
www.petershamnurseries.com
A lovely selection of plants,
containers, and pots in a beautiful
setting.

RE
Bishops Yard
Main Street
Corbridge
Northumberland NE45 5LA
01434 634567
www.re-foundobjects.com
Great shop and mail-order
company stocking interesting
bits and bobs suitable for gardens
and interiors.

RHS Garden Wisley
Woking
Surrey GU23 6QB
0845 260 9000
www.rhs.org.uk/gardens/wisley
Inspirational gardens and plant
centre stocking interesting plants
throughout the year.

Sarah Raven's Kitchen Garden
0845 092 0283
www.sarahraven.com
A beautiful selection of plants and
seeds, all available by mail order.

Sunbury Antiques
Kempton Park Racecourse
Staines Road East
Sunbury on Thames
Middlesex TW16 5AQ
01932 230946
www.sunburyantiques.com
A bi-monthly market selling a huge
selection of antiques and bric-a-
brac, where you are sure to find
all sorts of interesting pots and tubs
for the garden.

West Elm
209 Tottenham Court Road
London W1T 7PN
0800 404 9780
www.westelm.co.uk
Planters, terrariums, and garden
accessories.

UNITED STATES AND CANADA

Anthropologie (across USA)
(800) 309 2500
www.anthropologie.com
Ornate garden accessories.

Ben Wolff
305 Litchfield Turnpike
New Preston
Connecticut 06777
(860) 618 2317
www.benwolffpottery.com
Traditional and modern pottery
for the garden.

Fire Escape Gardens
(online/San Francisco)
www.fireescapefarms.com
Planters, seeds, tools, and
gardening accessories.

Grdn
103 Hoyt Street
Brooklyn
New York 11217
(718) 797 3628
www.grdnbklyn.com
A complete store for the
urban gardener.

Jayson Home
1885 N Clybourn Avenue
Chicago
Illinois 60614
(800) 472 1885
www.jaysonhome.com
Reclaimed pots and planters,
plants, container gardening.

Potted
3158 Los Feliz Boulevard
Los Angeles
California 90039
(323) 665 3801
www.pottedstore.com
Garden accessories.

Pottery Barn (across USA)
(888) 779 5176
www.potterybarn.com
Garden accessories.

Pure Modern (online/Canada)
(800) 563 0593
www.puremodern.com
Pots, planters, and garden
accessories.

West Elm (across USA)
(888) 922 4119
www.westelm.com
Garden accessories.

acknowledgments

A huge and heartfelt thank you to Debbie Patterson for such beautiful photography, for stamina, energy, and humor in all weathers, for beautiful props, and for supplying endless cups of tea and biscuits. Thank you to Gillian Haslam for such supportive editing and advice, Luana Gobbo for the lovely design of the book and for using my favorite shots so beautifully, Fahema Khanam for researching and booking locations and for remaining calm and understanding when the going got tough, and Anna Galkina for valuable help and assistance.

Thank you to Apta for the loan of the beautiful windowboxes and terracotta pot. Thank you to Alison Simcock and Tim Brown for the generous loan of the sink and for being undaunted by the logistics of transporting it. And a very big thank you to Cindy Richards at Cico Books, who, once again, has given me a wonderful opportunity for which I am extremely grateful. Finally, thank you to Laurie, Gracie, and Betty—for everything else. Thank you all.